THE STORY BEHIND

BREAD

Elizabeth Raum

Heinemann Library
Chicago, Illinois

www.heinemannraintree.com
Visit our website to find out
more information about
Heinemann-Raintree books.

To order:
☎ Phone 888-454-2279
💻 Visit www.heinemannraintree.com
to browse our catalog and order online.

Edited by Louise Galpine, Megan Cotugno, and
  Diyan Leake
Designed by Philippa Jenkins and Artistix
Original illustrations © Capstone Global Library, LLC
Illustrated by Gary Slater/Specs Art
Picture research by Mica Brancic and Elaine Willis
Originated by Modern Age Repro House Ltd
Printed and bound in China by CTPS

13 12 11 10 09
10 9 8 7 6 5 4 3 2 1

Library of Congress Cataloging-in-Publication Data
Raum, Elizabeth.
  The story behind bread / Elizabeth Raum. -- 1st ed.
    p. cm. -- (True stories)
  Includes bibliographical references and index.
  ISBN 978-1-4329-2346-4 (hc)
  1. Bread--Juvenile literature. I. Title.
  TX769.R346 2009
  641.8'15--dc22
                    2008037394

Acknowledgments
The author and publishers are grateful to the following
for permission to reproduce copyright material: Art
Archive p. **12** (Egyptian Museum Turin/© Dagli Orti);
Corbis pp. **5** (© Owen Franken), **6** (© Olivier Martel),
8 (© Bill Stormont), **13** (© Richard T. Nowitz), **16**
(© Minnesota Historical Society), **17** (© Hulton-Deutsch
Collection), **21** (© Anders Ryman), **25** (© Reuters/HO-
Mansoor Khalid/WFP), **27** (© Envision); Getty Images
pp. **4** (Iconica/© Tom Grill), **11** (The Image Bank/© Rita
Maas), **14**, **24** (© Brandi Simons), **26** (© AFP/Michael
Urban); Mary Evans Picture Library p. **15**; Photolibrary
pp. **iii** (Photodisc/© Jules Frazier), **18** (© PhotoDisc/
Buccina Studios), **19** (Robert Harding Travel/© Adam
Tall); Reuters p. **23** (© Mick Tsikas); The Bridgeman Art
Library p. **20** (© Giraudon/Lauros/Musee de la Ville de
Paris, Musee Carnavalet, Paris, France).

Cover photograph of hands kneading bread dough
reproduced with permission of Photolibrary Group
(Monsoon Images/Barry Pringle).

Every effort has been made to contact copyright holders of
any material reproduced in this book. Any omissions will
be rectified in subsequent printings if notice is given to the
publisher.

All the Internet addresses (URLs) given in this book were
valid at the time of going to press. However, due to the
dynamic nature of the Internet, some addresses may have
changed, or sites may have changed or ceased to exist since
publication. While the author and publisher regret any
inconvenience this may cause readers, no responsibility for
any such changes can be accepted by either the author or
the publisher.

Contents

Some words are shown in bold, **like this**. You can find out what they mean by looking in the glossary.

A World of Bread

 People have been eating raised breads for 6,000 years.

How often do you eat bread? Do you eat toast for breakfast? Do you have sandwiches for lunch? Do you ever have pizza for dinner? If so, you are eating breads.

Bread is a **staple**, or a basic and necessary food item. It can be made from different **grains**, such as wheat or rye. The grains are ground into flour and mixed with water to make **dough**. When the dough is baked, it becomes bread.

Raised breads

Most breads in the United States and Europe are raised breads. Bakers add **yeast** to the dough. Yeast is a tiny, colorless plant that makes the dough rise, or get puffy. People bake long loaves of French or Italian bread. They bake rounded loaves of white or whole wheat bread and square loaves of dark rye bread.

Money ✔

Some people call their work their "bread and butter." What they mean is that the money they earn keeps them alive. Today, the words *bread* and *dough* are both used to mean money.

Flat breads

In other parts of the world, people prefer flat breads. In the Middle East, from Egypt to Afghanistan, people like a soft flat bread. In Egypt they call this bread aesh. In Syria, Lebanon, and Yemen it is called khoubz. (*Khoubz* means "bread" in Arabic.) In India people eat a flat bread called naan. Tortillas and tacos are flat breads eaten in South and Central America.

▼ **This Turkish woman bakes flat bread in an outdoor oven.**

5

Growing grains

Bread is made from grains such as wheat, rye, corn, or oats. The process of growing and **harvesting** wheat, rye, corn, or oats is very similar.

Wheat is the most widely grown **cereal** grain. Wheat fields cover vast areas of the United States, Russia, China, and Europe. Common wheat (also known as bread wheat) is used for making bread, cereals, and pastries. It grows in areas where there are mild temperatures and fewer than 76 centimeters (30 inches) of rain per year. Other kinds of wheat, such as the durum wheat used to make pasta, can grow in colder climates.

▼ Farmers in Nigeria, Africa, prepare to harvest their wheat fields.

Why eat bread?

Bread provides **nutrients** that the human body needs to function and stay alive. Bread contains **carbohydrates**, which give the body energy. According to food experts, adults should get about half of their carbohydrates from whole grain products. Children need carbohydrates, too. How much they need depends on their weight and age.

Bread also contains **proteins** that help the body stay healthy. B **vitamins** are found in bread. These help break down the carbohydrates and proteins so that the body can use them. Bread provides **calcium**. Calcium helps strengthen teeth and bones. Fiber is a part of wheat that helps the body digest food and get rid of waste.

Bread in many languages

The word *bread* comes from the Old English language. Germans call it *Brot*. The Dutch say *brood*. People in Denmark call bread *brøt*.

▼ This chart shows world wheat production in 2007–2008.

Nation	Amount of wheat produced (in thousand metric tons)*
European Union**	119,646
China	106,000
India	75,810
United States	56,247
Russia	49,400
Pakistan	23,000
Canada	20,050
Kazakhstan	16,600
Argentina	15,500
Iran	15,000
World production	**604,961**

*1 metric ton = 1.1 tons

**The European Union is composed of 27 European countries.

From Fields to Tables

▲ On large wheat farms, machines called combines harvest the wheat.

Farmers plow (turn over) the land, plant the seeds, and then wait for wheat to grow. Just before the wheat is fully ripe, farmers **harvest** it. First they cut the stalks. Then they separate the **grains** from the straw (see diagram). This is called **threshing**. **Combines** do this work on big farms (see box). On smaller farms, threshing may be done by hand.

After the wheat is harvested, it is sifted and the grain is loaded onto trucks. Sometimes it is stored in giant towers called **grain elevators** until trains or trucks take it to the flour **mill**.

Combines ✓

Combines are huge machines that cut the wheat and separate the grains from the straw. They also sift it and load it onto trucks. U.S. inventor Samuel Lane designed the first combine in 1828. In 1890 it took 40 to 50 hours of labor to produce 272 kilograms (600 pounds) of wheat. By 1975 it took only 3.5 hours to do the same work, thanks to better combines.

▼ This picture shows the parts of a grain of wheat and how it grows on the stalk.

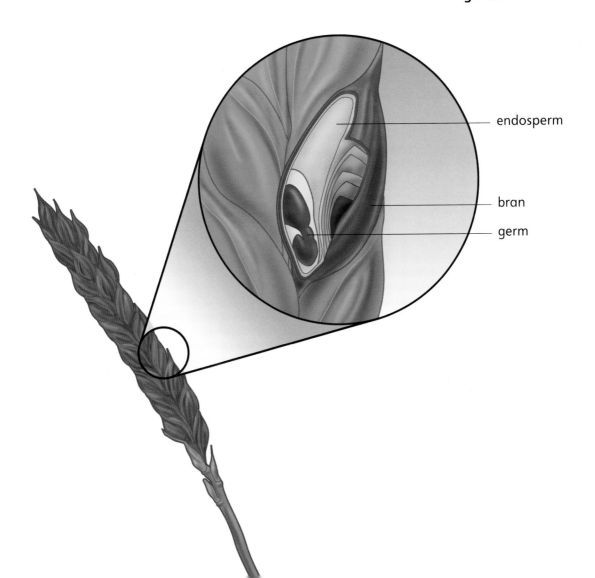

endosperm

bran

germ

To the flour mill

At the flour mill the wheat grain is inspected to make sure it is good quality. It must be dry. Damp wheat gets moldy or rotten. The good wheat grain is stored in silos. These are large containers shaped like cylinders.

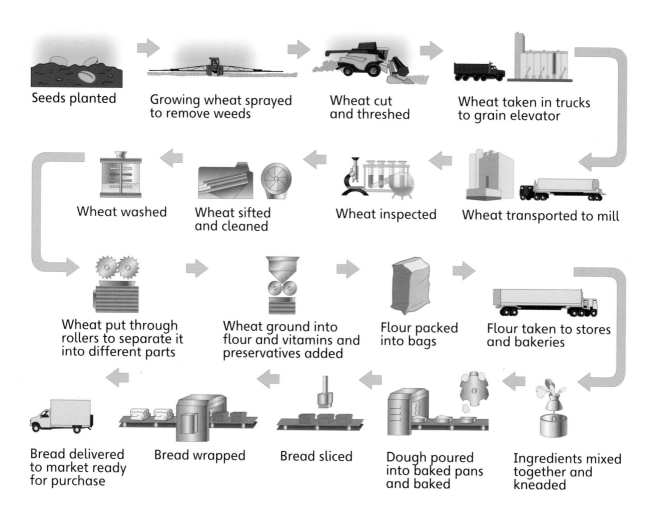

Seeds planted

Growing wheat sprayed to remove weeds

Wheat cut and threshed

Wheat taken in trucks to grain elevator

Wheat washed

Wheat sifted and cleaned

Wheat inspected

Wheat transported to mill

Wheat put through rollers to separate it into different parts

Wheat ground into flour and vitamins and preservatives added

Flour packed into bags

Flour taken to stores and bakeries

Bread delivered to market ready for purchase

Bread wrapped

Bread sliced

Dough poured into baked pans and baked

Ingredients mixed together and kneaded

▲ **This diagram shows the process of making bread, from sowing the wheat to delivering the sliced loaves.**

When a miller (a person who works in a mill) is ready to make flour, the wheat grain passes through a series of metal screens. The screens remove objects such as sticks and rocks. Then the grain is washed in warm water and spun dry.

In large mills, two big rollers crack open the grains of wheat. Machines separate the different parts of the grains. Different parts make different kinds of flour. Wheat flour is made from the endosperm of the grain (see diagram on page 9). Most bread is made from wheat flour. Large metal rollers grind the grain into flour. Different chemicals and **vitamins** are added. Then the flour is packed into bags for delivery to bakeries and stores.

To the bakery

To make the simplest flat breads, bakers add water and salt to the flour. For raised breads, they also add **yeast**. Recipes for fancier breads may also include eggs, butter, sugar, and milk. The ingredients are mixed together and poured into baking pans. After the bread is baked in an oven, it is cooled and sliced.

Mix-ins

Bakers add all sorts of ingredients to breads. Nuts and fruits are popular. Ingredients such as cinnamon, dill, or garlic give bread a different flavor. Some breads include bits of meat, olives, cheeses, onions, or peppers.

▼ **Yeast makes bread rise. It may be fresh or it may come in dry form, as in this picture.**

A Short History of Bread

▲ Art like this sculpture teaches us about ancient Egyptian bread making.

Early people hunted and fished for food. As they moved from place to place, they gathered plants growing in the area. These people probably ate **grains** such as barley, oats, wheat, or rye that they found growing along riverbanks. At first they ate the grains raw. Later they boiled or roasted grains.

The first farmers

In about 7000 BCE (about 9,000 years ago), people in what is now Iran and Syria began farming grain crops. Over time, they learned to make bread. The first breads were probably flat breads cooked on hot stones.

7000 BCE
Growing grains begins in areas that are now Syria and Iran.

5000 BCE to 3700 BCE
Grain becomes a **staple** food in Egypt and spreads to Europe.

7000 BCE   6000 BCE   5000 BCE   4000 BCE

In Egypt, women using water from the Nile River discovered that their bread would become puffy. Nile River water contains **yeast**, which causes bread to rise. No one knows exactly when this happened. But ancient Egyptians painted pictures of loaves of raised bread on tombs about 5,000 years ago.

Ancient Greece and Rome

The ancient Greeks enjoyed bread, too. About 3,000 years ago, bakeries in Athens sold 72 different kinds of breads and cakes. Ancient Romans learned from the Greeks and soon made rounded loaves. Roman armies spread their bread-making skills throughout the continent of Europe and to Great Britain.

Paid in bread

The slaves who built the pyramids were given bread as payment. In Rome, bread was given to the city's poor. By 250 CE, Romans gave free bread to 300,000 people.

◀ Ovens like this from the ancient city of Pompeii, Italy, were used all over Europe.

3000 BCE	**1000 BCE**	**55 BCE**
The Egyptians make raised bread and invent the closed oven.	Bakeries flourish in Athens, in ancient Greece.	In Britain, the Romans introduce better ways to make bread.

3000 BCE	2000 BCE	1000 BCE	0

Watermills and windmills

Watermills existed in China 1,000 years ago. But they did not reach Europe until much later. The first windmills in Europe were built in northern France about 1,000 years ago. Soon, windmills were built in Germany, Holland, and Britain. Both watermills and windmills were used to grind grains for bread making.

▼ For hundreds of years, windmills like this one were used to grind grain.

500–1450
Bread becomes the most common and essential food in Europe.

0   500

Rich and poor

White bread is made of the most finely ground flour. During the Middle Ages (500–1450 CE), only very rich people could buy white bread. French breads became famous throughout Europe, where people grew to love white bread.

Guilds

In the later Middle Ages, bakers formed **guilds**, or unions. Before guilds, rich landowners owned the ovens. Guilds allowed bakers to own their own ovens. Guilds also made rules about baking and controlled the price of bread.

◀ Guilds prevented French bakeries like this one from raising prices too high.

During the 1500s, several wars, **epidemics** (widespread diseases), and **famines** (times when food is scarce) made life especially difficult. During bad years, only rich people ate bread made of wheat. Poor people ate bread made of straw, clay, and ground tree bark. They made cakes from acorns or crushed roots. Many starved.

Trenchers

During the Middle Ages, rich people used bread as a trencher. A trencher is a kind of plate for meat. Juices from the meat soaked into the bread. When they were finished eating, they often tossed the bread to the servants to eat.

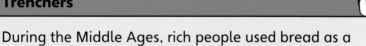

1000
Watermills are used to grind flour in Europe.

1100s
Bakers are organized into guilds.

1000

▲ This 1926 photo shows workers using a bread-slicing machine.

Otto Frederick Rohwedder

It took U.S. inventor Otto Rohwedder many years to invent a machine that sliced bread. He began work on it in 1912. By 1928 his machine sliced bread and wrapped it to keep it fresh.

The Industrial Revolution

By the mid-1700s, better farming methods and machines brought times of plenty. Famines and epidemics were less of a problem.

Life began to change. A new engine run by steam provided power for other machines. These machines took over much of the work that people had done by hand. This shift in the way people lived and worked is called the Industrial Revolution.

Farms using tractors and **combines** required fewer workers. People moved from the country to the city. They worked in factories. Life in the cities was difficult. Without farms or garden plots, city workers no longer grew fresh foods. They had to buy their bread.

mid-1700s
The Industrial Revolution begins in Britain.

1700   1750   1800

Industrial ovens

At first, most bread was made in small bakeries. As time went on, bigger bakeries bought better ovens to bake faster and more easily. Small bakeries could not compete. Many went out of business.

Bigger bakeries meant lower prices. Even poor people could buy white breads that used the best flour.

By the 1900s, some bakeries froze and reheated the bread **dough**. Some used poor quality flour. Many breads lost their taste and flavor. In the 1940s, food experts began to add **calcium** and **vitamins** to bread to make it healthier.

▼ This 1935 photo shows workers loading bread onto a delivery truck.

1849	**1870s**	**1928**	**1941**
The first industrial bakery opens in the United States.	Large-scale bakeries open in Britain.	Otto Rohwedder invents a bread-slicing and bread-wrapping machine.	Calcium and vitamins are added to flour to make it healthier.

1850   1900   1950

Celebrations

▲ This bride and groom are breaking a loaf of braided bread called challah.

Many celebrations include bread. People eat bread at parties and family get-togethers. Birthdays, holidays, and weddings include special breads or cakes. So do funerals.

Wedding breads

In eastern Europe, some weddings feature fancy breads molded into the shape of a heart. The bride and groom bow in front of the bread. They kiss each other. Then they break the bread and hand it out to their guests.

In Poland, bread prepared for a wedding may be decorated with doves and flowers. The bread reminds wedding guests that the best gifts are peace, plenty, and happiness.

In some areas of central Asia, the entire village attends each wedding. Everyone brings specially baked breads or sugary flat cakes. In other parts of Asia, the bride's family gives squares of fried **dough** to each wedding guest.

Olney Pancake Race

A pancake is a form of bread that is fried rather than baked. There has been a pancake race in the town of Olney, England, every year since the 1400s. People race through the streets with frying pans. They toss a pancake in the air at the start of the race and again at the end. In 1950 the town of Liberal, Kansas, held its own race. The two towns now exchange visitors on race day each year.

▼ This is a loaf of wedding bread from the Greek island of Crete.

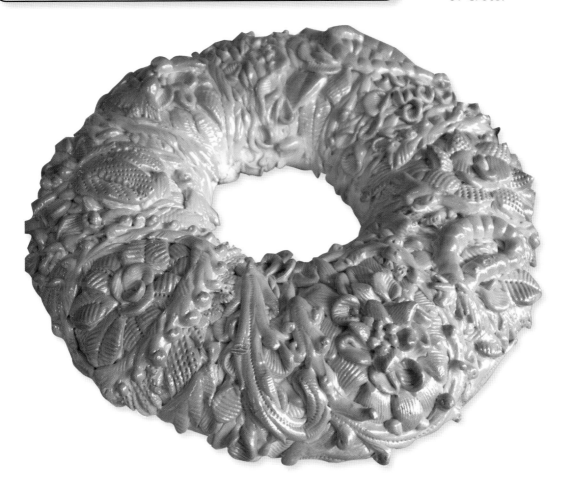

▶ This bread is part of a harvest celebration.

Harvest festivals

Throughout history, people have celebrated their **harvests**. Every August, people in Ireland celebrate Lammas, or the Celebration of Bread. It occurs just after the first wheat harvest. Americans wait until the harvest is complete to celebrate Thanksgiving. Wheat is often used as part of Thanksgiving decorations.

In the Czech Republic people celebrate Obzinky. After harvest, farmworkers make wreaths (circular arrangements) of rye, wild flowers, straw, or ears of wheat. Young girls wear the wreaths on their heads. They parade through the town. Everyone dances and eats.

Funeral breads

In ancient times, bread was buried with the dead. When scientists explored the pyramids in Egypt, they found loaves of bread that were 3,500 years old. Even today in some areas of Pakistan, a bag of bread and cheese is buried with the dead. Until the 1700s, French villagers gave bread to the poor whenever a rich person died. This custom reminded villagers to work together during difficult times.

Bagels

A Polish legend tells the story of Jan Sobieski, king of Poland. In 1683 the king rode on horseback as he led his troops to save the people of Austria from attack. A local baker made bread in the shape of a stirrup to honor the king. He called it *beugel*, the Austrian word meaning **"stirrup."** People loved the new roll. Over time, the shape changed to a circle with a hole in it—the bagel.

◀ These bread dolls, created to celebrate All Saints' Day in Bolivia, South America, remind people of relatives who have died.

Is There Enough Bread?

Today, there are almost seven billion people in the world. It takes a lot of bread to feed that many people. Is there enough? Will there be enough in the future?

People have always celebrated in times of plenty because they know that sometimes they do not have enough. For many people in the world today, there is not enough to eat. In the early 21st century, periods of bad weather have hurt wheat crops throughout the world. The United States and Australia suffered droughts, or lack of rain. In Europe, floods have hurt crops. These problems lead to rising prices for bread and other foods.

▼ This chart compares wheat production in 2005 and 2007, showing how it has gone down.

Nation	2005 wheat production (in thousand metric tons)*	2007 wheat production (in thousand metric tons)
European Union**	132,356	119,646
United States	57,280	56,247
Canada	25,748	20,050
Australia	25,173	13,100
World total	621,305	604,961

*1 metric ton = 1.1 tons

**The European Union is composed of 27 European countries.

Higher prices

Higher food prices could push 100 million people into poverty. People in African countries such as Ghana, Nigeria, and Zimbabwe are hit especially hard. In February 2008, 11 people died in Egypt as they waited in line to get bread. Most died from heat exhaustion or heart attacks. Two men were stabbed when a fight broke out.

In many poor countries, bread prices more than doubled in 2007. Even in the United States, where there is no food shortage, food prices are rising. Experts expect costs to keep rising. Poor people throughout the world feel this increase the most.

Bread is king

"Bread is the king of the table and all else is merely the court that surrounds the king."

U.S. author Louis Bromfield (1896–1956)

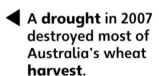

◀ **A drought** in 2007 destroyed most of Australia's wheat **harvest**.

Fewer farms

In many countries, land that used to be farmland is now used for factories, highways, or housing. This has happened in Japan and China. Both countries now buy **grain** from Australia, Canada, and the United States. Today, Japan buys 70 percent of its grain from other countries.

Bread or beef?

Poor people get over half their daily food needs from grains such as wheat, rice, or corn. As incomes rise, people eat more meat (beef or pork), milk, and eggs.

People in North America and Europe use far more grain per person than people in poorer countries. But people in these countries are not eating more bread—they are eating more meat. Meat comes from animals that eat grain. The animals need lots of grain to grow big and strong before they are killed for their meat. So, it takes lots of grain to produce meat.

▼ **It takes lots of grain to feed cattle.**

What can we do?

Some experts believe the answer is for everyone to eat less meat. It may be easy for one person to change, but it is difficult to convince everyone to do it.

Other experts believe farmers need to improve the way they grow crops. Scientists are studying ways to improve seeds, protect croplands, and provide water in times of drought.

▲ These children in Afghanistan depend on grain from other countries because of a serious drought in their country.

Turkey likes bread

Turkish people eat more bread per person than people in any other country. They eat an average of 200 kilograms (440 pounds) of bread per person every year.

Sandwiches and Dinner Rolls

▲ The base of a pizza is a kind of bread.

We eat bread every day. **Cereals** are among the first foods babies eat. As we grow older, we may have toast or bagels with breakfast, a sandwich for lunch, and a roll or a slice of bread with dinner. There is bread coating our chicken strips or fried fish. Salads often include toasted pieces of bread called croutons. Even our desserts—cookies and cakes—are a kind of sweetened bread.

The sandwich

John Montagu, the fourth earl of Sandwich, did not want to stop playing cards to eat. One day in 1762, he put slices of cold meat between two slices of bread. This is how the meal got the name sandwich! Sandwiches became popular in Britain. They soon spread to other countries throughout the world.

◄ People in the United States and Europe eat about half of their bread as sandwiches.

Bread has a long history. White bread used to be only for the rich. Today, everyone can choose white bread. In recent times, however, many people have returned to whole **grain** breads. Doctors believe that whole grain breads are healthier.

Bread is so common that we seldom think about it. Millions of people work hard every day to grow the wheat, **mill** the flour, and bake the bread we eat. Hard work puts bread on our tables.

You decide

Every day people make decisions about what they will eat. Will they choose to eat more grains and less meat? Will they share their grain with other nations or store it up for themselves? What do you think are the right decisions?

Timeline

(These dates are often approximations.)

8000 BCE
In Egypt a simple grinding stone, called a quern, is used to create flour from **grain**.

8000 BCE

3000 BCE
Natural **yeast** in the Nile River creates raised breads. The Egyptians invent the closed oven.

3000 BCE

4000 BCE

1000 BCE
Raised bread is popular in Rome.

2000 BCE

1000 BCE

1100 CE
Bakers are organized into guilds.

1000 CE
Watermills are used to grind flour in Europe; flour is sifted, leading to finer white bread.

1600

1000 CE

1683
According to legend, the bagel is invented in Austria.

1870s
Large-scale bakeries open in Britain.

1849
The first industrial bakery in the United States is opened by businessman W. B. Ward.

1828
U.S. inventor Samuel Lane designs a **combine** for **harvesting** wheat.

1912
U.S. inventor Otto Rohwedder begins work to invent a bread-slicing and bread-wrapping machine. (He finishes it in 1928.)

1936
Ancient loaves of bread are found in an Egyptian pyramid.

1941
Calcium and **vitamins** are added to flour to prevent disease.

1900

This symbol shows where there is a change of scale in the timeline, or where a long period of time with no noted events has been left out.

7000 BCE

Farmers in Syria and Iran begin growing wheat.

7000 BCE   6000 BCE

5000 BCE to 3700 BCE

Grain becomes a **staple** food in Egypt and spreads to Europe.

5000 BCE

250 BCE

People in Rome receive free bread from rulers.

150 BCE

A bakers' **guild** forms in Rome. Wealthy Romans eat white bread.

55 BCE

The Romans invade Britain and introduce better ways to make bread.

0

500–1450

Bread is the most common and essential food in Europe.

mid-1700s

The Industrial Revolution begins in Britain.

1700

1762

John Montagu, the Earl of Sandwich, invents a new way to eat bread.

1800

2000+

Weather causes bread shortages. Bread prices increase.

2000

Glossary

BCE meaning "before the common era." When this appears after a date, it refers to the time before the Christian religion began. The Christian religion is counted as starting at year 0.

calcium a natural element that builds strong bones and promotes heart health

carbohydrate substance produced in green plants that provides energy when eaten. Wheat is a good source of carbohydrates.

CE meaning "common era." When this appears after a date, it refers to the time after the Christian religion began.

cereal edible grain such as wheat, rye, oats, rice, or corn. Today, many cereal grains are eaten for breakfast.

combine harvesting machine used for cutting and threshing grain in the field. Horses pulled early combines.

dough flour or meal combined with water, milk, and other ingredients that is then baked. When dough is baked, it becomes bread.

drought period of dry weather that can damage crops. Recent droughts have hurt wheat crops in Canada.

epidemic disease affecting many people at the same time. Epidemics killed many people during the Middle Ages.

famine lack of food that causes extreme hunger for many people. Bad weather can destroy crops and cause famine.

grain cereal grass such as wheat, corn, rye, oats, rice, or millet. Bread is made from grain.

grain elevator large storage container for grain. Most grain elevators are located near railroad tracks.

guild union of workers in a particular job. French bakers all belonged to the bakers' guild.

harvest gather a crop from the field; also, the season when a farmer gathers crops from the field. Many farmers use combines to harvest wheat.

mill grind grain into flour; also, a building where grain is ground into flour. Grains must be milled after they are harvested.

nutrient something that helps the body grow strong and healthy. Bread contains nutrients.

protein any of a large number of substances present in milk, eggs, meat, and other foods that are a necessary part of the diet of human beings and animals. Protein helps the body grow and repair itself.

staple basic and necessary food. Milk, eggs, and breads are staples.

stirrup metal loop that you put your foot into when riding a horse

thresh separate grains of wheat from the straw. Combines cut and thresh wheat.

vitamin something found in natural things such as raw fruit, dairy products, fish, or meat that is needed for a healthy body. Bread contains vitamins.

yeast a tiny, colorless plant that makes bread dough rise, or get puffy. Flat breads do not need yeast.

Find Out More

Books

Bentley, Joyce. *Everyday Food: Bread*. Mankato, Minn.: Chrysalis, 2006.

Jones, Carol. *From Farm to You: Bread*. New York: Chelsea House, 2002.

Sertori, Trisha. *Body Fuel for Healthy Bodies: Grains, Bread, Cereal, and Pasta*. New York: Benchmark, 2008.

Websites

Visit the Cyber Toaster Museum.
www.toaster.org/museum.html

Visit a Cyber Space Farm to see a wheat harvest in Kansas.
www.cyberspaceag.com/visitafarm/photoessays/wheatharvest/default.htm

Learn more about the history of bread.
www.kitchenproject.com/history/Bread/

Take a look at the Food Timeline.
www.foodtimeline.org

Explore the Grain Chain.
www.grainchain.com/7-to-11/The-grain-chain/Default.aspx

Places to visit

Visit a wheat farm or a bakery.

Visit a grocery store and check out the wide variety of breads now available.

Index